breathe with me

with me

using breath to feel strong, calm, and happy

Mariam Gates

ILLUSTRATED BY
Sarah Jane Hinder

sounds true
BOULDER, COLORADO

You are always breathing
up and down,
in and out.

You use your breath each
time you talk or sing,
for every whisper and
every shout.

Your breath can be short
and quick like the drum line
in a marching band.

Your breath can
be long and slow
like waves rolling
onto the sand.

You will breathe 25,000 times today and that is healthy for you.

But do you know what else your breath can do?

One deep breath in and one long breath out can make you feel better too!

If you are tired in the morning and it's hard to get out of bed,

use Rainbow Breath to get your body moving and wake up that sleepy head!

Rainbow Breath

Sit up and let your spine grow tall.

Bring your arms out straight to
the sides, palms down.

Inhale and sweep your arms up over
your head, palm to palm.

Exhale and bring your arms back
straight out to the sides, palms down.

Repeat three times.

When you go somewhere you've never been and you aren't sure what to do,

you can use Dandelion Breath to feel more comfortable trying something new.

Dandelion Breath

Sit up and let your spine grow tall.

Imagine a soft dandelion flower.

Take a deep breath in
and then blow the air out slowly,
sending the seeds into the air.

Repeat three times.

When something makes you
mad or even feels unfair,

try Counting Breath and
you'll feel calmer there.

Counting Breath

Sit up and let your spine grow tall.

Take a deep breath in, counting silently 1 . . . 2 . . . 3.

Then let your breath out, counting silently 1 . . . 2 . . . 3.

Repeat three times.

Sometimes you may be sad
and feel like crying too.

A gentle Belly Breath can help
when you are feeling blue.

Belly Breath

Lie down on your back.

Place one hand on your chest.

Place your other hand on your belly.

Take slow deep breaths and feel your
chest and your belly move up and down
as the air goes in and out of your body.

Repeat three times.

At night, when it's hard to fall asleep because your mind is busy and your body feels tight,

try Balloon Breath to get relaxed and ready for a good night.

Balloon Breath

Lie down on your back and let your hands
rest by your sides, palms up.

Inhale through your nose and imagine filling
your body with breath like a big balloon.

Exhale and blow the air out
through your mouth.

What color is your balloon?

Repeat three times.

Your breath is always here for you
in a calm and quiet way.

Use it to help you choose
how you want to feel
in each moment of your day.

With one deep breath in
and one long breath out,
you are on your way!

For Mila,
My little breath of happiness.
SJH

For Jasmine T. Gates
MG

Sounds True
Boulder, CO 80306

Text © 2018 by Mariam Gates
Illustrations © 2018 by Sarah Jane Hinder

Published 2018

Book design by Meredith March

Printed in South Korea

Library of Congress Cataloging-in-Publication Data

Names: Gates, Mariam, author. | Hinder, Sarah Jane, illustrator.
Title: Breathe with me : using breath to feel strong, calm, and happy /
    by Mariam Gates ; illustrated by Sarah Jane Hinder.
Description: Boulder, CO : Sounds True, Inc., 2018. |
    Audience: Ages 4-8.
Identifiers: LCCN 2018013102 (print) | LCCN 2018032722 (ebook) |
    ISBN 9781683640516 (ebook) | ISBN 9781683640301 (hardcover)
Subjects: LCSH: Breathing exercises—Therapeutic use—Juvenile
    literature. | Relaxation—Juvenile literature. | Child mental health.
Classification: LCC RM733 (ebook) | LCC RM733 .G38 2018 (print) |
    DDC 615.8/36—dc23
LC record available at https://lccn.loc.gov/2018013102

10 9 8 7 6